If I Were a Bumblebee

To my mother, for giving me the courage.

To my children, Grady and Morgan,

for giving me the reason.

I Love You!

Printed in the United States of America

First Printing, 2021

ISBN 978-0-57886-540-9

Library of Congress Control Number: 2021903957

Visit the author's website www.ifiwereabumblebee.com

If I were a Bumblebee,
I'd tell you what I'd do...

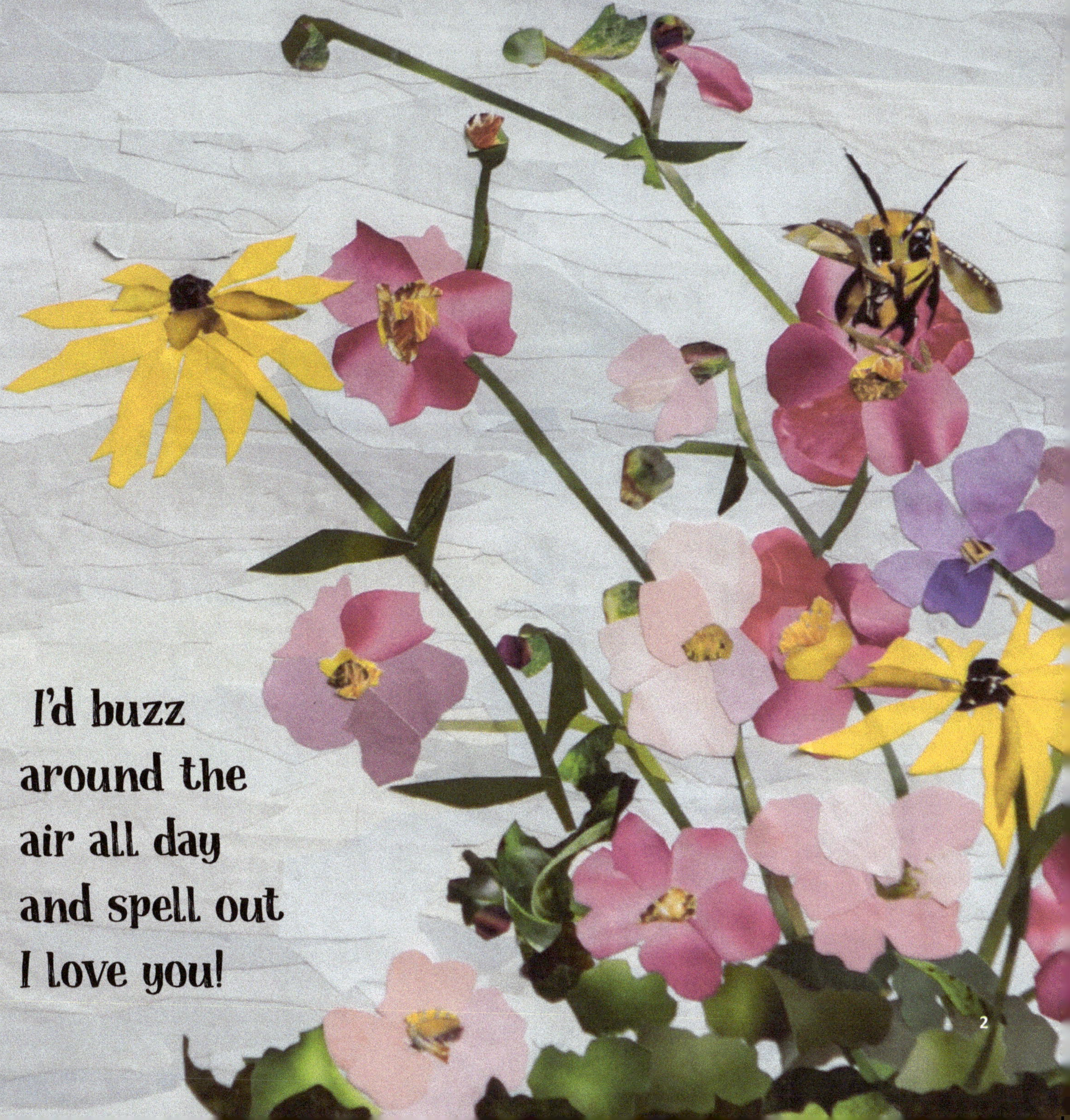

I'd buzz
around the
air all day
and spell out
I love you!

If I were an old Sand Crab,
I'd tell you what I'd do...

I'd crawl around the beach all
day and spell out I love you!

If I were an Arctic Hare,
I'd tell you what I'd do...

I'd hop around the mountain top
and spell out I love you!

If I were an Ocean Wave, I'd tell you what I'd do...

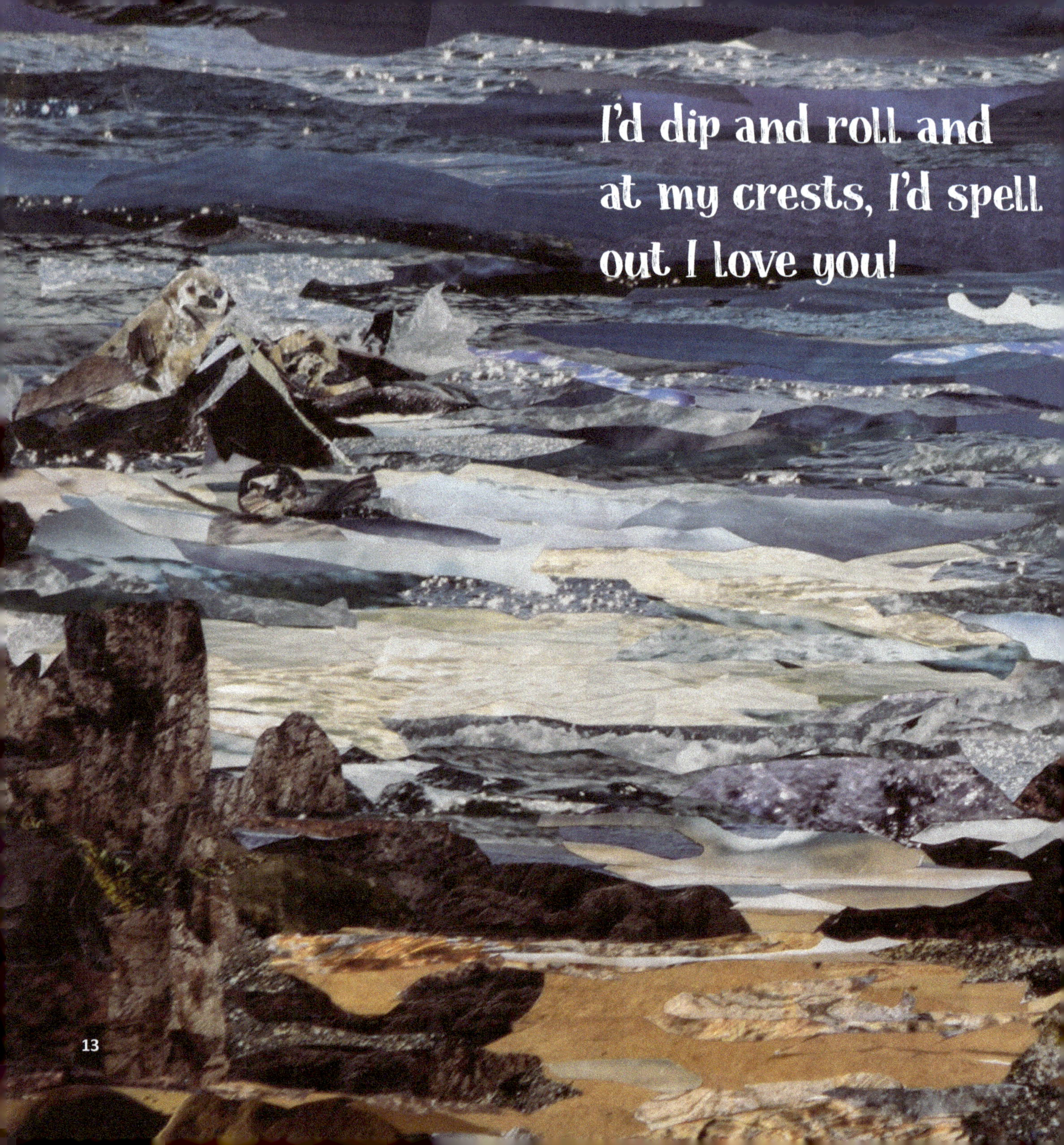

I'd dip and roll and
at my crests, I'd spell
out I love you!

I broke you!

14

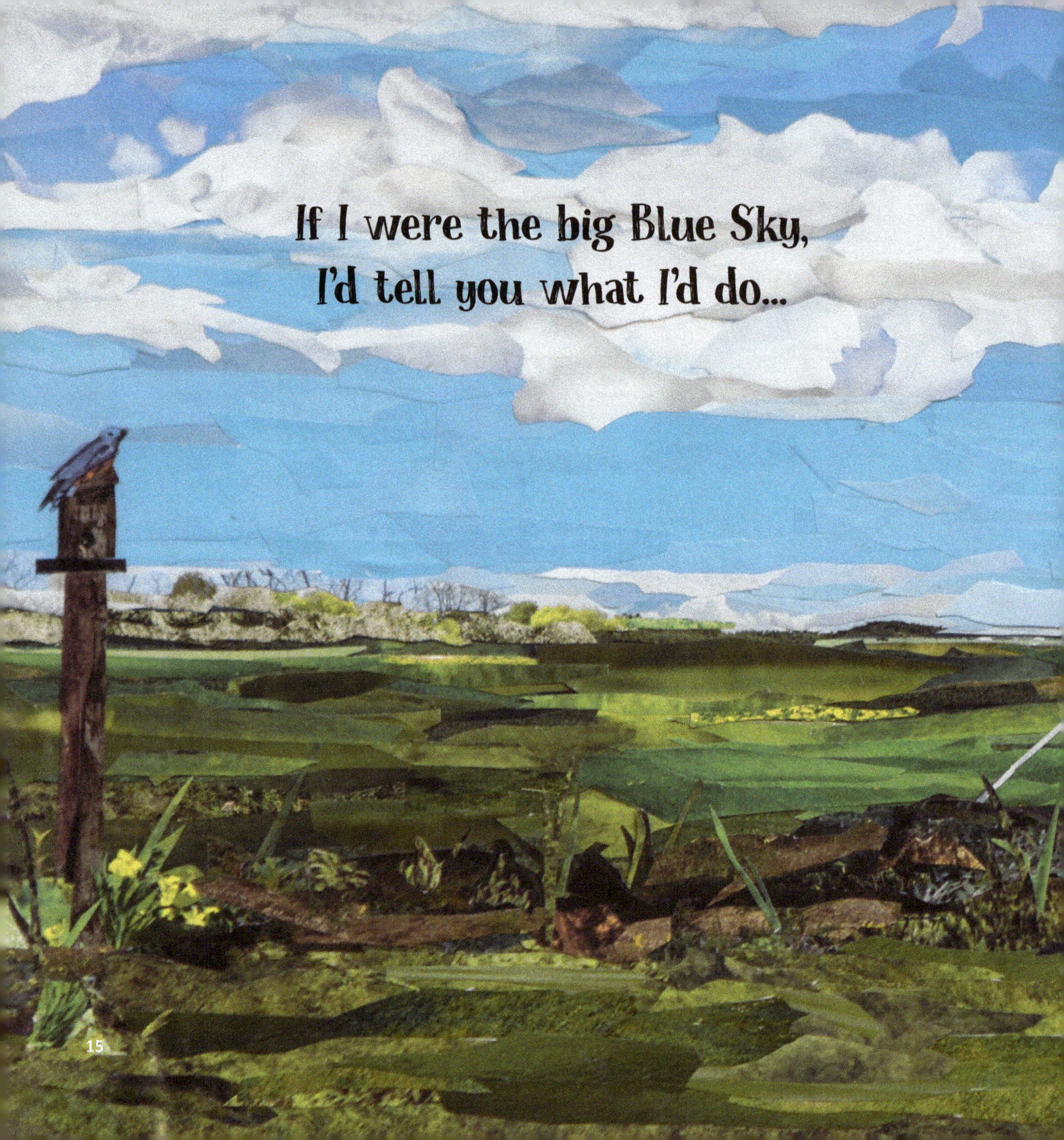

If I were the big Blue Sky,
I'd tell you what I'd do...

I'd gather all the fluffy clouds
and spell out I love you!

But since I am your loving mom,
I'll tell you what I'll do.

I'll hug and kiss you every
day and tell you...

I love you!

www.ingramcontent.com/pod-product-compliance
Lightning Source LLC
Chambersburg PA
CBHW040926050426
42334CB00061B/3481